Wile & Wing

poems

Kimi Sugioka

Manic D Press
San Francisco

For my son
Kai Sugioka-Stone,
my collective family, and all poets
who cull their words from the brambles of truth

Some of these poems have appeared in the following publications in slightly different forms: *Poetry San Francisco*; *Bombay Gin*; *The Once and for Almanack*; *Exit Zero*; *Big Rain*; *A Spawning of Protons*; *Gathering of the Tribes*; *13th Moon, Vol. XV*; *Glass House in a Hurricane*; *Standing Strong! Fillmore & Japantown*; *Endangered Species, Enduring Values: An Anthology of San Francisco Writers and Artists of Color*; *Civil Liberties United: Diverse Voices from the San Francisco Bay Area*; and *The Language of Birds*.

The author thanks all of the people who have given their love and support throughout this project. My son, Kai Sugioka-Stone, who lights my heart path; my chosen and blood family, Stephanie Sugioka, Marla Weber, and Susan Dambroff, who continue to believe in my right to write; Kathleen Au and Mia Ruiz, who helped me birth and grow this manuscript; and my publisher, Jen Joseph, without whom this book would have not have been conceived or completed.

Cover artwork: John Fadeff

Published by Manic D Press, Inc. For information, address Manic D Press, PO Box 410804, San Francisco California 94141.
www.manicdpress.com   Printed in Canada

CONTENTS

vermillion whispers
buffalo cloud sunrise
trampling the sky

Rites of Passage

Come friend or foe
the dice is only as loaded
as the throw

Beguile me with
beatitudes
and infinitudes
of prayer and melody

That we may become whole
despite the
circumference of injustice

Deities may embrace
the few
but birdsong
is for all

That which brings peace
begets peace
a moment of home
must sustain

Though our sons may wander
realms so distant as to
eclipse the thin walls
between us

Destiny resides
in the palm
of creation

Where we reconcile
madness with love

Core

Was it Eve's
after she consumed
the flesh?

Core from chorus:
a melody the wind sings
through bamboo groves
and apple boughs

Song of wings
scatterings of seed
from the womb
the craven mystery
that relinquishes its grasp
once felled

Perhaps an angel
cloud or dirt
devil muttered
between barnacle encrusted pilings
the likes of which we chant
in harmonious cacophony
limbic and visceral

Core:
that which differentiates
bone from meat
embedded
in nether worlds
where we tango
and pray
that teeth might
masticate

that tongue might
remember
the forgotten kingdom
of apples

The woman breathes

her breast swells in
dream in
detritus in
perilous
fracture

The woman holds
the child
the long spoon
the tired baby
the old man's hand
the worry
like a kettle
on a 400,000
-year-old fire

The woman arranges
flowers
spices
contrives
encounters
decoys

The woman sings
with scythes
and sibilant
ruminations

She toils, sweats
becomes
one of the many
her
incarnate

presence
addresses
calamity
with temperance
and nests inside
morning
creates prayer
with scimitar
and samovar
erases the blood stains
over and over

She of nightingale
and anaconda
radiant
empath
and soldier
blazing blues and
radical orations
of the precocious grey whale
the gregarious grey wolf
seeking sanctuary
creating sanctity
with breath

Half Privileged

Half Japanese
Half Scots-Irish
Half upper middle class: coca-cola in the fridge,
tempura or roast beef on the table,
apple pie in the oven

Half neglected: garbanzo beans, olives or popcorn
scavenged because my mother was too broke or broken
to shop or cook
Half North Carolina demure
half California dissident
half exotic lily, merchant marine pin-up girl
half loved

Half privileged to go to college, get by
inherit enough for a condo down payment
half terrified of not being able to pay the mortgage
but making sure to buy twenty pairs of socks
for my son so he won't get the bleeding feet
I had as a child
because of the one pair of socks I wore all week

Half self-absorbed and self-indulgent
half plagued by madness, depression, and guilt

half nihilist   half optimist
half stubborn   half acquiescent
half brilliant   half broken
half penitent   half impudent
half teacher   half poet
half sinner   half seraph
half you   half me
half otter   half tree

Half salmon
     swimming
          out to sea

Wildfire

The sky weeps words
        soaking prayers
                drenching dreams
to quench the unquenchable
        thirst of flame

        Rain
Water
        Hope
Reason
        renounced in smoke

People and creatures flee
Trees ruminate and explode

Time becomes
            a larder
            a cauldron
            a mosaic

Tile upon consecrated tile
endures
        escapes
            ensnares
each weighted breath

crisp feathered morning
ashes of sleep scatter
murmurations of starlings

Isis and Maat

Thin weeds of misperception
are woven into the dawn of Isis
and sunset of Maat
How many rings
must circle Saturn
before the goddess
speaks?

The bartered
internal hammerings
of core and mantle;
mutterings
of the lethal and
the winged

Combining mythologies
with traces of mutton and milkweed
Answers to
virtual prayers

I, the princess
I, the sorceress
I, the crone
Amplitudes of
taupe and rose
crescendo in
fists of resistance

I didn't come here to prevaricate
I didn't come here to abstain
I came for the moment of dewfall
The cries of intemperate children
The flight of pelicans, butterflies
and kestrels

For it is they who slay us
with keenest vision
without vested interest
in credit or trade
with violent pasts
and bleak futures
who come by love
without judgment

If it wasn't for them
there would be
no reason to embark
on this heretical odyssey

Meeting Gwendolyn Brooks

She'd come cross-country
on a train 'cause she didn't
trust hollow metal bodies with wings
to Boulder, Colorado
to read and greet
the new poets at the
Jack Kerouac School
of Disembodied Poetics

We had lunch together –
some students and a teacher –
as we gawked and sputtered
something half-heartedly
half witted
she suddenly stopped
and looked from one
to the next
through her long worn
stained and history steeped
glasses and asked
*Where are your dark skinned
poets?*

Everyone looked at me
like I was suddenly
representing all the
absent colors
The teacher volunteered
She isn't well and couldn't come
as though that might do

I wasn't so much upset
by Ms. Brooks' question

but embarrassed as I
failed to be
dark enough
to make up
for all those absent
blossoming
minds

It is a question that
remains unanswered in
the Norton anthologies
and *New Yorker* magazine

It was a great honor
to meet
Gwendolyn Brooks, I still
have a battered
autographed copy of her
Selected Poems
still read
We Real Cool
to some of my
more wayward
charges

Knowing that Gwendolyn
paid overtime, double time, and
time and a half
for her slice
of literary pie

Ms. Brooks
finished her lunch
and paid the bill

The Poem Burlesque

The only thing
I am wearing
is a few

sequined
syncopated
tasseled
disclosures

my buxom
pantoum

my only conviction

Let me
entertain you
with

these nuanced
illuminations
these subtle
alliterations

my seductive
sestina
and
surreptitious
word hustle

My only
offering, my
only
choice

In Memory of Allen Ginsberg

You echoer of Whitman, Blake, and Williams
seeker of sexually transmitted enlightenment
You always asked me, "How's your heart?"
and gestured towards the nearest young man
saying, "Won't he do?"

You belligerent buddhist word breeder
queer anti-nuclear activist
cushion-sitting macrobiotic diabetic
My last gift to you, a diet Sprite at a backyard barbeque
You soul-shimmying, kewpie doll-headed singer of "Father
    Death Blues"
dope smoking, acid taking, dream mongering swindler
You compassionate and generous of broken old men
Ignorer of women's writing
Your last gift to me, a pink octopus drawing

You idolator of pretty boys
the paradox of you so demanding of negative capability
that it cuts and scrapes its way into the belly
gnawing away all the platitudinous properties of western duality
to sew the heretical seeds of Dionysian plurality

You babblingly brilliant blabbermouthed
self indulgent "first thought, best thought" non-editor
prophesier of pathological apocalypse within the spirit of this
    nation
doomsayer, breath taker, million-mouthed buddha slayer

I am pink with grief
because you were supposed to stay with us forever
or at least until we died
and you were so big

bigger than your photo on the Gap billboard
smiling and haling us into San Francisco
big enough to fill my world

Don't blame me for this poem
You were the one who always said,
"Candor ends paranoia"

Strawberry Angel
for Dominique Lowell

breaks open broken
        hearts and sings
                the scarlet and indigo
of Ariadne
        Andromeda
                Antigone
who await her with westerly winds
        and northern gales
while they do
                hard time as archetypes
        her poems pearl
in oyster and spiral shells
                in a tidal zone
you hold to your ear
        where you might hear her
                and believe her
                        an ocean

With mini-skirted thighs
        the shape and size
                of a child's she sends
                        a shaft of moonshine
                down our spines
        breathes and breaks
                into jack o'lantern grin
poker-faced and whiskey laced
        she fights
        with double fisted
                foul mouthed
eloquence
        and always counts to ten
                before taking the literati out

              and trouncing their
ivory towers
              into tinsel-town
                            souvenirs

Strawberry angel
              what griffins and dragons
                            lashed you to
              King Cobra's tongue?
A forked hiss is all he can give
              while you can crack
                            the whip of a waxing moon
                                          straddle her crescent and swing
                                                        like a hoodlum
throwing bottles and rocks
              and back talk
                            till we laugh
no, howl
              at you who woo
                            so well
in your wild-eyed way
              a barfly
curandera

Why Not?

Remember the unthinkable
speak the unspeakable
tell tales of the dead
until they squirm and spin
in their graves

Why not be
recklessly wise
humbly audacious
foolishly sublime?

The connections slither
like water snakes
between us
barely visible
wildly infused and
alliterated by
one another

Why not
smash the imaginary panes of self
shed the scales
so we might see
might touch
might hold
might correct our use of pronouns
no more I, he, she or they
only we?

We the creatures
We the fir tree, sweet pea, and madrone
We the stones and the river
We the cow and the farmer

We the swallow and the raven
We the bone and skull of ancestors
We the homed and homeless
We without predicate
We who long for one another even
in the stench and filth of steerage
on this one boat
this one passage
this one planet
this one universe

Why not?

Ghostship

Arrangements
      cannot be
made
like a bed
or a grave

When the young
      die from attending a warehouse party
          amidst the chaotic radiance
of dismembered art
      in stacks and layers
      in towers and alcoves
      tunneled between pianos
      bicycles, madonnas, skulls
decorative toilet bowls and clawfoot tubs
         torn velvet curtains and ancient
            Persian carpets

The chance one takes
      to assemble dreams from
scrap metal and knickknacks

to be an artist
      in Oakland
in the 21st
century

Stacking the Deck

Moments are stacked
in a deck of hours
in a box of days
with hearts of sky
souls pass by
sheltering minutes
months or years
before moving on

Explanations only prolong
departure
stringing beads of dusk
with filaments of song
tertiary algorithms
eclipse pentatonic melodies
with twilight
eccentricities

Just before folding
a winning hand
all the one-eyed jacks
went wild and
left for parts unknown
and here we are
all alone

backward knees
bad haircut, bold strides
arrogant egret

Sweet Nothings

I have decided to whisper sweet nothings into your ear tonight
'cause it's all I really know how to do
I learned early from the maid who took care of me
when my mother could not
a black woman who knew
the weight and size and shape of color
in Moncore, North Carolina

I didn't know what color I was —
my birth certificate said "white"
but I was an almond-eyed anomaly
born into the whiskey-laced womb of the South
to a white mother and a Japanese father
whose animosity for one another
clawed well past color and culture

Not that I could see color
till I moved to Berkeley, California
onto Telegraph Avenue
in 1965
I mean I saw it in the picture shows *Gunsmoke* and *Wagon Train*
where I mistook myself, not for the Indian princess,
but the blue-eyed blonde

It must have been the humidity

But that's a long time ago
I have been identified as native —
Navajo, Cherokee, Hawaiian, Eskimo —
in the eyes of my beholders for so long
I finally gave up and invisibly claimed that heritage
proud to wear the hair and eyes of the disenfranchised
and the wiser for walking those irrefutably ambiguous borderlines

Here I am
knowing nothing
so well
I can practically
taste it

God and the Badger

Bent and venerable
    long-bearded and robed
        staff and bindle in one hand
            sacred scroll in the other
God may be a carved Chinese man,
    standing on the mantle
        one ear to the wind

Noseless and footless
    big bellied and saucer hatted
        a carved Japanese badger
    accompanies him
flat-eyed to the sun

They have traveled together
    for 70-some years
Witness to
human transience
    and intransigence:
    the blighted marriage
        the blue Danish sofa
            the births of four babies
    before
a murder of tea-leaf printed plates
    flew across a pinewood kitchen
    after
the chrysanthemum hilted samurai sword
    once unsheathed in a marriage scuffle
        slipped from the hand
            the blunt hilt mashing
                the mother's big toe

The 200-foot-tall pine tree
        toppled by lightning
the onerous laying of Carolina slate patio and fire pit
        and stringing of many hued Japanese paper lanterns
                in preparation for boisterous oyster parties
the annihilating humiliations of the firstborn son
the long journey from Carolina to California
the mother's smokeless death by lung cancer

The strange pair kept company
        in the picture-windowed Chapel Hill home
                in a pink stucco Telegraph Avenue apartment
                an Oakland hilltop tree house
                        a bungalow next to the 580 freeway
                                a Queen Anne Victorian basement
                a Raymond Carver condominium
on the shores of Alameda

Witness to
histrionics, despair, death, and birth
    smuggled kittens and biting dogs
but the pair only
        shrugged as they shuffled from one vignette to the next
the bashful, stoic badger
the old man obliviously absorbed in his mission
        to deliver the precious scroll

Though bonding by proximity was
                                inevitable
        they never spoke or invoked
affection

Gone the mother
        gone the father
                and childhood home

                    Only god and the badger remain,
          hardier it seems
than homes or lives

Witness to
          the scraping and scooping gestures
                    of toilers with empty cups
          filled with blessings
filled with dust

Only god and the badger
          survive the crushing weight
                    of so much
          absence

Sacred Profanities

Now I lay me down to sleep
may the stars spill from
subway pockets
and convince the Milky Way
to spill all the secrets
you kept from me

      I pray the earth my soul to keep
      since you are the singer of
      Sumerian lullabies, sing me
      Inanna, Queen of Heaven and Earth

If I should die before I wake
may the baby Jesus
I made from acorns
and placed on a cross of twigs
exonerate
all that is wanton
and shamed

      I pray the dust my soul to take
      in a drenching rain
      with fire all around

Guide me to know
which tales to inhale
which ones to blow
through like Winnemucca,
Nevada
thumbing rides
red-eyed
barefoot and tuxedo clad and
oh so low
and dry

If I should live another day
may I know
what the sky knows
but only tells the birds
what the ocean knows
but only tells the whales
what the trees know
but only tell one another
in root tongues
underground

Aleuchi

It's just that I don't trust hospitals
where honey-skinned men are concerned or
manzanita women for
that matter considering
Billie Holiday
and so many
others

Killer King hospital took one such
beautiful young man
I met when he was maybe 9 or 10
exceptionally human
and
brilliantly
alive
I
remember
the
Rodney King insurrection
his mama said he drank
so much orange soda he
got a stomach ache
and she
laughed
through the
chaos and
worry

At the age of my own
beloved son
bicycling across the
country Aleuchi
fell sick in LA

where he was
stashed in a back room
alone with
a curable illness
no one to hold
his hand or
advocate
for the poem
of his breath
until his phone
and life lost their charge

A story
I didn't believe
was mine
to tell until
so many
years
passed
and so many
dark-skinned
young men
became
the ghosts of
so many
cherished
children

Just the facts, ma'am
Just the one truth that
trumps all other truths
the one that doesn't fade
fray or rot
in my throat
like a bone

or a bird
without wings

To wake with surging pulse
and breathe without fracture
the way Aleuchi finessed
a day into
fluted moments
a perpetual
blossoming and scattering
of unstrung
pearls
feathers
bubbles
raindrops
humming with
everything and
nothing at
once

Pelicans

Squadrons of brown pelicans
wing westward and loll
in the Alameda estuary
20 to 30 at a time

Up to six feet of beak
descendants of Dalmatian ancestors
wend through 30 million years
only minutely evolved
laconically speaking to friends
and silently slaying the sky

Reminding us
not to lose faith because
not all flight is armored

Not all winged creatures
have been changed or
broken by human betrayal

Not all humans want
to desecrate and
commodify nature

Some
just want to watch
pelicans
fly

Public Transportation

When I was 6 or 7
and wore my hair in braids
I became part of the spectacle
in Boone, North Carolina
on the Tweetsie Railroad
Wild West theme park ride
along with tanned & buckskin clad
actors waving tomahawks
as the train passed by
all the little alabaster kids
ran up asking
"Are you an injun?"

> *A spider parachutes*
> *on a puff of wind*
> *that carries it from tree to tree*
> *or across oceans*
> *weaving a singular strand of silk*
> *connecting past and future*
> *and you to me*

Above the BART platform
a jelly-faced waxen man
calls down
to three cinnamon princes
he throws them a bill and yells
"It's great to see you guys
dancing on the train
instead of killing and
robbing people"

> *The lodgepole pine among others*
> *can only reproduce*

when fire melts the resin
in serotinous cones
that release its seeds

At the San Francisco airport
I wait for a plane
with Jésus who
while walking through a
restaurant
almost drops a tray of dirty dishes
shoved into his belly
by a stone-eyed Texan

> *We carry the vision and*
> *wisdom of our ancestors*
> *like seeds deep beneath*
> *our skin*
> *try to embrace a*
> *middling existence*
> *climb propitious ladders*
> *that lead to storm drains*
> *beneath the feet*
> *of the elite*
> *hoping for a glimmer*
> *of human recognition*

A mourning dove-hued father
cries about the times
he has witnessed his adopted
mahogany child walk into a corner store
to buy candy
as the shopkeeper
bristles and growls
as though the little boy has
already committed a crime

Like rabbits
in a field of low grass
we seem too terrified
to meet the gaze
of the being
beside us
despite our familial
solicitude

An ashen-skinned poet tells me
that I'm not anymore
Japanese than he
that my heritage has been
bleached from my skin
through assimilation
never acknowledging the generational
scars left by persecution, incarceration
and silence

The proliferation of
seedlings
can only be cannily
awakened
by the purifying
flame

On the train, the guerrilla dancers
flip and tumble
in gyrating double-jointed
grace
they are carnival joyous
just shy of raucous
knowing their place
all too well

Remember
the spider's
audacity
and the strength
of her
filament

The Tiger

The hotel was immense
corridors and balconies
floor upon floor
of room upon sterile room

Only the tail was visible
in moments
as I wandered alone
wondering where
and when he would find me

Every corner and corridor
a miter of life and death
It wasn't till I finally knew
there was no choice
that I turned
to see those dear tufted ears
those ephemeral eyes
the elegant slope of his back
that I knew
I was home

Liminal Migrations

from cell to shining cell
mawkish
brain fodder
hubris
traces
of ancestors
flushed from
the wound in
a parched sunrise
where streets
change direction
every second moon
and we are
no match
for the quick-witted
flicker or
red-tailed hawk

in the city's crush
ring and ram of winter night
a full rabbit moon

One Life in Two Parts

1.

Before my son
I twinkled, twiddled, danced Caribbean
dreamt in Greek
ran with the bulls of whimsy
spun and stumbled
spit and mumbled
riddled with words that spilled like fountains of nickels
from the frozen, frothy muzzle of a carousel horse

I was here for the ride
discipled to word
song and circumference
Listened to Van, Bruce, and Bob
like there was no tomorrow
never dreamed tomorrow
was another day

no down payments
strictly cash and carry
and I took only what I could carry
I wasn't into love nests
hearth and home tests
I was up till 3 and slept till noon
yackin' and crackin' wise
swooning and waxing that big
poem in the sky
my lullaby
my syncope
my salud y dinero

I was sculpting and molding
each day as it came

it was bonafide
pay as you play
and pay
and pay

Don't get me wrong
I wasn't a rocker or a dime bag doper
I wasn't a reefer suckin' cold duck smoker
No, I was more of a moper and all the time
was dreamtime
studying the path of the Green Ant and
the Red Road
always late
or giddy
with the guilt of the
self-condemned, I the
poet
prosecutor
jury and judge

2.
After my son
I climbed on that pony
and held on tight
learned to wake
to someone else's cries

I was asleep by 9
up by 6
(and 2 and 4 and maybe more)
I was sleep walkin', workin', and payin' dues
to the babysitter, doctor, baby gym proctor

The world suddenly shifted
from solipsism to rock-hard work

It was work to eat
eat to work
navigating cries
of hunger
cries of pain, or just plain
too tired to cope
we both just sat down and wailed
like hound dogs
in baleful pleas
for some kind of peace

He cried
I cried
we all cried
for three long months
until he smiled
the wide and worldly wondrous smile
of one who'd fought and won
his painful withdrawal from
my anti-depressants
the ones they now say
may cause grave neurological damage
to the fetus

And I tried to become the mother
I never had
as one determined
to build a castle
with only a vague intuition
of structural architecture

But there I was
parenthood upon me
like a hurricane on a sparrow
and suddenly there was no time

for dreaming and moping and
reading and writing
or even dressing —
it was all I could do to
take a shower
with my son strapped into
some baby contraption
beside the tub

I, with the starring
role of supporting actress
without lines or rehearsal
to improvise
and roll in the muck
of every kind of human fluid
learned to become fluidly
human

And so it was
he grew me up
taught me the true measure
of sacrifice
that somehow still wrung
the dew from the roses
at dawn

Wedding Psalm

The silvery dust
of wing and hoof and paw
settles in gentle revelry
the fleece of 25 years floats
about your shoulders

From the croon and sway of Muddy Waters
to time eloquently ebbing
in the tidal purge of all
that ever clung or burned
leaving wisps of melody
and parable

Your feathers honed
from the vedic stamens of lilies,
wistful trills of
cello, piano, accordion
and winsome calls of cormorant and osprey

Homed beside the murky waters
of Clear Lake
and the crystalline waters
of Blue Lake
you homed yourselves
sweated and baked your trials and terrors
into tenable
misgivings

Homed
wayward cats
that respect the rights
of bushtit and hummingbird
to eat and bathe
within claws' grasp

Homed
the abandoned horse
and fire-driven fox
in menagerist
circumference

Holding some fire
some hearth of mantels
that winnow and shuffle
motes and neurons
into an archipelago of
unique and universal
belonging

The Recipe

The walls are
sobbing, coughing
retching, raging, yelling
shaking with moans and laughter

I make salad —
romaine, carrots,
pears, chives

The recipe
is handed down
from generations of
ghosts in the kitchen

I see the eyes
of a street dying man
I see the eyes
of a perpetrator
I see the consequence of
unsheltered
innocence

Last year I complained
about the birds
waking me at dawn
twittering, singing
telling lies and stories
  finch and sparrow
  junco and robin
I complained
and now they
are all gone
except for the crows

Decisions about circumcision —
if an infant is greeted
with sexual stimulation
followed by mutilation
then what are the
repercussions when
he becomes a man?

Cucumbers, arugula, mushrooms

I chop and cut
pondering the
ontological imaginings
of honey bee
and wolf pup

Microcosm
Macrocosm
the front door speaks volumes
to the man
in a tent
on the sidewalk
in 26° weather

Whether or not
we agree
on a perspective
what is cannot be
denied

Crow people,
why have you become so abundant?
why have you replaced the others?
why are the grebes settling on the north shore
of Clear Lake?

Now when I hear one bird sing
near my window
I am feathered
with remorse

The mail comes in droves
of unsolicited
advertisements
I didn't know that I didn't want
a roomba
and can't distinguish the favorable properties of one
humidifier
in an avalanche of humidifiers

Comparison shopping
chopping garlic, celery

A toilet
no matter what the line and hue
flushes shit
away

Adding lemon juice, olive oil
double cheddar
flailing gestures

A gorilla
signs
  save the earth
  help the earth
she says that she
loves humans
even though
we are stupid

The earth protests
gently at first
  fires, floods, tsunamis, a slow
  species extinction
and like the starving mother bear
with starving cubs
she will slay us
so that she may live
to procreate
another day

Sprinkle thyme, rosemary, dill

What is the next
ingredient?

Descant on the Faces of Love

In the mirror of night
my true nature
sings and arcs
above infraction & censure

The text of despair
erased and retooled
with wit
with artifice
refracting into
disrepair
in the name of
Silence
to atone for the cacophony
raging between the pages
of my sins

descant
descent

into a skinwalker's greed
I, of lust and determination
am the shadow
in his path

where berated souls
bloom false-petaled,
vagabond intimacy

and shatter the mirror
or the illusion
of the mirror

Having slung the moon
in the left side pocket
I have come
with crystal plate
and crusted spoon
Namesake
Keepsake

Slaker of thirst & longing
for wounded gods
with broken tongues
my heart is a penny
in your boot
to remind you
of the price
one pays
for love

Beauty is Truth

The curled fist of an infant
the flophouse rumination of beleaguered old men
the pining murmurs of young love
fingers ferreting chords to mimic
the menacing and mirthful cawing of crows
that mingle with memories of a long dead mother
in a singed tuft of longing
to mine stories out of the ether
and stir them into the daily fare
of bean and barley soup

The siege of predictable and familiar events
the teenager's boredom at family gatherings
unremarkable mutterings between beasts
one bellow, one phrase or syllable
might liberate a singular meandering echo
that reifies the spirit and illumines revolution
and leads us simply and sublimely
home

the work of silence
evokes stillness and star fall
implicating myth

Infusion

Something to place into water for tea:
    chamomile, ginger, mint, or
to make the air radiant with fragrance:
    rosemary, eucalyptus, lavender, or
to flush into the veins:
    Sodium Chloride, Retuxin, Benadin, Deximethazone

Rows of recliners replete with reluctant, slack, sleeping
    or impatient patients
IVs, shunts, and ports attached to calibrating boxes that
beep loudly and often
demand the attention that the patients don't
sometimes exceeding the number of nurses
available to answer their cries
disconsolate as hungry infants

Warmed cotton blankets
compensate for the overly air-conditioned pod
speckled grey linoleum floors
white paneled ceilings with random paintings:
butterflies, roses, and an underwater scene of seahorse, octopus,
    clownfish,
and a school of sharks

The patients — bipedal or with canes, walkers, wheelchairs
or on bone-thin legs — file in
with smiling, sad , preoccupied or dour faces
A nurse says admiringly,
You still have muscle after all you've been through

Most of the nurses are white-skinned
most of the attendants are dark-skinned
it doesn't really matter that this is Virginia

the demographics are pretty much the same
everywhere in the USA

But here come Judy and Trent
in their 60s or 70s
he has a James Brown kind of cool
dark glasses that never come off
she castigates Trump with the chirp of a house finch
18 years he's been coming here
twice heroes, cross-racial and married
in the Jim Crow South
battling cancer with chemo every month

Dozens of dancing solar-powered flowers, Santas, cats,
   scarecrows, dogs, bears, bees, butterflies
line the window sills
simpering with the simple herculean strength
of sunlight

Sonata
for my father

Mellifluous
somber, soothing
phrases
emerging
and receding

A note of reminiscence
a note of disdain
a note of hysteria
(a demented 7th or augmented 5th)

Knotted notes
to unwind in prayer

Nestled notes:
the three-year-old
patting your face and saying
I'll see you tomorrow
when tomorrow is a moment
or an eternity away

Thready notes
that cling tenaciously
to the tonic
impeccable notes
that are carefully but unwisely
rendered
repeated and held notes
that retrace the palm
over and over

Redolent notes
after wine and sympathy

Incandescent notes
that live in fear
of their own demise

Idolatrous notes
that cannot bear
to behold their own
reflection

Golden-slippered notes
that clatter mindlessly
across the floor above

Tidy notes
that sweep and scrub

Sonorous notes
that pitch and reel
in nuanced
resonance
of prelude
and coda

The tender threnody
of a life
declined

Queen of Diamonds

Mothers actually come in coveys —
  one brings you coffee in bed
  one laughs till she cries
  another cradles your baby
  a fourth wipes away your tears
when brambles become tangled
with the honeysuckle vine

I wear a golden chain that was once
my other mother's
On the chain I wear a Hawaiian sea-colored pearl
that you gave me on my 50th birthday

Along with classical maternal teachings
  cooking and sewing
  apple pie and
  Julia's randy roast chicken
  interfacing
  before it became a cyber word
you taught me hem and bias
the tension of thread just so

You believed all women
should cut their hair short at 30
and fussed over my long tresses
and unkempt locks

You came when my son was born
and when he was sick
you nursed my father
until the years shook him loose
like a stone
to rest in his rock garden

You are the mother of plans and errands
  bridge playing and beach walks
  monopoly and contract rummy
  my brothers' home fire
  my son's darling granny

I may be a one-eyed jack
but you are the queen
of diamonds

Sisters

The miles unfold in chaparral, piñon, and red sage
Denver to Trinidad to Raton to Santa Fe to Albuquerque
clouds purl over red sand
like escaped genies
from ochre mesas and charcoal arroyos

In the Casas de Sueños we swallow our senses
and converse in the language of the lost
No longer 7 & 12
now 57 & 62
we weep with the loss of the Issei
the Nisei
and the dream of one another
these past 50 years

We struggle to assimilate our assimilation
in this America of cultural annihilation
this family of internalized racism
the Hiroshima Sugiokas decimated
the California Sugiokas scattered

We try to stop erasing ourselves
with intra-generational silence

Leaving the South

The land of thick, green
rivers, red clay, and sweltering
undergrowth
Tennessee Williams territory
Carson McCullers
Robert Johnson
Dorothy Love Coates
Flannery O'Connor
John Coltrane
ghosts
line up like mantel postcards

Humidity hovers like a lover
over jasmine hung white pillared mansions
not far from human auction blocks
and the flower ladies
of Franklin Street

Wisteria whispers
meanders and twines
meadow and cloud rapture
fly the edge of innocence
like a hummingbird egg
in a crow's beak

Panoply of six minds
  one fallacious
  one hellacious
  one charmed I'm sure
  one desolate
  one drunk on mint juleps
an amalgamation of contradictions
dwelling inside the one tee-ninsy brain

Damaging moments
make for disparate departures —
We must leave it to the dead
to absolve the living

The Staunch White Moon

You of familial calligraphy
tainted daybreak and long
suffering dusk

You who worship
Calliope, believing
she can transmute all
that love leaves in skeletal ruins
on a crust
of crumbling earth

See how the staunch white moon forgives
the stars' shimmer when it falls
from earth's rim
and acquiesces
to cricket song

This inky betrayal
a silent dirge
before daylight frowns
into an ever receding
wedge of egrets

Try to remember
four or four million years, past or future
flickering like candles strung
on the great ridge of night
and despite her departure
a thimble of
moonlight brazenly shines within
the wizened blue-rimmed eye of a
buttery caged cockatoo
speaking purple-tongued dulcet hellos
in a veiled plea
for freedom

American Dream

The smoke in summer
simmered over California like a
semaphore
melting the sky
like burnt butter

Scorched sentience
hallowed
by thy name

The earth reclaims
herself
in flames
and hurricanes

Humans scuttle
like roaches
up the walls of
the American dream

volcanoes simmer
hemispheric lullabies
turtle island sleeps

Stories

unfurl like soiled
blankets
the misfit
child
the underdog
janitor
the angry
teacher
insinuated
parables

I come home with groceries
to a cold dark condo
bereft with the infestation
of school district bureaucracies
that disregard humanity
and favor
intransigent colleagues
who believe that humiliation
begets remorse

I feed the cats and rabbit
carefully minding their
delicate digestive tracts
eat cheetos, olives and m&ms
for dinner

The boy runs and grins
Will you chase me?
growls, pouts
punches the air
and kicks the basketball pole
avoiding answers

to addition and subtraction
an angry caricature
his voice a wildish whisper
the other children ignore
mimic or misunderstand

An invisible man
sweeps, mops, scrubs
the feces from
the bathroom stalls, walls
and floor
where disgruntled
employees
prolifically shit
in myopic protest of
policies and practices
over which he has
no control

He listens acutely
to tunes and news
while
endlessly coughing
the toxic dust
of an unventilated
post office warehouse

Weary and wearier
we walk the plank
of self censure
a vapor
of elocution
of grit and gravitas
a fragile mooring
in a harbor of

maelstrom
tired
targeted
imperfectly equipped
to manage the slipstream
currents and eddies
of our lone
quests and missions

but when
the teacher toggles
the child and the child
embraces the janitor
the stories become
interlocked
the way a poem grasps
and sometimes
raptures
and in moments
is complete

Therie

has a phone number
no shopping cart
a thin blanket
sits in a doorway on 14th Street
I gave her $5 and she
thanked me
said she enjoyed talking to the people
at Fisherman's Wharf, Germans and
people from other countries were
kind and nice and she
has a friend who might give her a
job detailing cars
and if I wouldn't mind taking her number
in case I hear of a job or
a place to live
maybe I could call her
to let her know
and I took her number
walked
to my car wondering
what good $5 will do
when she's sitting on a
piece of cardboard
without warmth or
protection and
might not survive
the coming storm
but I got in
turned on the heater and
drove home

Tomorrow I will
return to my job as a

school teacher
and try to manage the
borderline abusive
borderline psychotic teacher
who, with the expertise of a seasoned puppeteer
has the whole district administration
tap dancing on razor blades
and I will do the best I can
to protect the children
one more day
from another broken
system

Paraprofessionals

This is what
you do when someone calls you a name
This is what you do when you feel angry
This is what you do when you feel like running away
This is what you do when you feel like your head is exploding
This is what you do when you come to school

Where skeletons of best practice
socio-political trends and fads
hover in every doorway
blocking the angels
of spontaneity
and joy

In the hallways, classroom corners, drafty breezeways
with stories and stickers, charts and fidgets
the women come armed to shape and conjure
flexibility and resilience
in angry, rigid, and anxious children

There are children who scream
who refuse to move from the corner
they have chosen to occupy for eternity
wailers and criers
runners and kickers

The paraprofessionals
    paid much less than the underpaid teachers
arrive with certainty, clarity
that these impossible feats
will be accomplished

I have watched these women
living paycheck to paycheck

or on money they borrow or give to each other
fiercely initiating, advocating, insisting
on the right of these children
to co-exist with their "normal"
classmates in classrooms where

The teachers
complain or cannot contain
their frustration and shame
when these children erode
their painstaking plans
to instruct the other 24 or 30
in things no child would want to
learn in the oppressive costume
of common core standards

No more nap time in kindergarten
no fingerpaint, or field trips
no more exploring, wondering
pondering the path of an ant
the bark of a tree
no running, no climbing, no and no and no
music, no art, no science

Just the teachers and
a few mental health workers to
field the rising tide of
frustration, anxiety, and despair
and the paras
who bravely go where no
principal, school administrator, or
superintendent
would dare

Iris

Forty-eight 7- and 8-year-old voices consecrate
the crud-gray multipurpose room with
love, joy, pride, visibility
first and second grade children
sing *A Million Dreams*

except Iris
exiled, denied
because she didn't do
her homework
and lies
about everything
even her grandmother:
  can't breathe…
  in the hospital…
  dying…
  the church…with people

You have to
fill in the blanks
provide the words:
  oxygen, funeral, prayer…
she isn't able to
coherently lie
in a language
that marbles her tongue
warbles her speech

Iris
doesn't participate in
class activities
sits apart
won't share

acts like she
doesn't care
like she doesn't
want
to learn
even though
she has been trying
to master
the sounds
and sinister
configurations
of English
syllables
for three of her eight
years

Maybe she could sing
maybe she could stand
and mouth gibberish
maybe she could
move her hands
in emulation of
the ones who
know how

The class prepared for a month
at every rehearsal
Iris was sent
away to work on
synonyms and definitions
far beyond
the scope of her
vocabulary and lexile
or made to sit
and watch

her classmates
practice the song
they would sing
for the senate and governors
of their world

It's 2019
a native Spanish
speaking
so-called
learning disabled
child —
a brown skinned
girl of 8 —
is excluded
reduced
to feeling less
than her tribe
less than
her culture
less than
the songbirds
just beyond the
school walls
that sing
at will

Why We Need Smaller Class Sizes

You can never tell who will make the connection —
     it might be the music or PE teacher
     the reading or speech specialist
     the principal or crossing guard
There are so few of us
and so many of them
How can two hands hold 25?

How can one mind contain these multiple realities and remember
     to speak gently to the shy one
     assertively to the bold one
     hold the hand of the frightened one
     to keep the one who pinches from the one who cries
     to speak concisely to the ones just learning English
       just wrenched from their homes in ravaged countries
     with a tone of respect to the angry one
     to honor all with words that kindle
     the will to learn

There are children who can't keep their hands out of their mouths
because their teeth are rotting and their parents
can't afford a dentist

Or those who
     can't see
         the board
because their glasses are   broken
and the insurance only pays for one pair per year

Or those who throw chairs and run

Have you ever tried to convince a child
after years of failure
that she can succeed?

Have you ever tried to do your homework
when you are homeless?

Have you ever had to call Children's Protective Services because
a child showed you where his mother bit him
or the cuts and bruises from when his father smashed
his head on a car
or discover a child's long sleeves on hot days
cover cigarette burns that run up and down his arms
or because a child whispers about something her uncle did
that left her broken?

Have you ever tried to teach a child who is the only person in the
family who isn't a junkie?

Have you ever tried to explain inference to an audience
of five different cultures
who speak five different languages
none of them your own?

I don't have
the money to pay
for the child who is hungry
the one with rotting teeth
the one who can't see

I sometimes know
how to help them persevere in the moment
I don't know
what happens when they leave
A wise psychologist told me
a child learns for love before they can love to learn
But it's hard if the only love they know doesn't meet their most
basic needs

There is only so much a teacher can give
The librarians, nurses, counselors, psychologists, music and
 art teachers
have dwindled to a handful

There is only so much time
to listen
to appease

These first few years are our only chance
to teach purpose, action, and practice
to prepare them for
the unknowable
future

Bird Island

This moment
        That pelican
                moored to wind
                        gliding cliff-ward
40 years of erosion

So far
        from muddled streets
                and a lonely death in the backroom
of a welding shop
                where a father halfway scrawls
                his daughter's number
                on a paper
                by his bed

Someone to call
after you're gone
        without handwringing or
        hospital tubes

I know the wrack of wind
        and sea weary rock
A scattering of feathers
        in a lifetime of waves

Some stray day
                we play
for the sake
        of arcing across the sky
                above a sea
                        where a buoy
                rings like church bells
        signaling

sanctuary

Just leave

      The breath
            a monument
to life

Colossus Unbound

On land bequeathed
     by millennia of intrepid grace
standing in vestige remnant
     a shamed steel skeleton
in tarnished copper jawed
     shock

shining
     gold leaf light

on the high-heeled and shoeless
     tenacious or contemptibly blithe
haunting and hunted
     on tenterhooks
in floundering facsimiles
     of freedom
in the wake of
     the leviathan:

     Send these, the homeless, tempest-tost…
the lost, the hunted,
the reprieved
     the wretched refuse of your teeming shore

Let us be done with
     these imaginary borders
     and heed the fading echo of Emma's din —
Let them in!
Let them all in

The Meaning of Kai

Yoruba, Hawaiian, Maori: sea
Greek: earth
Scottish: fire
Chinese: open
Japanese: restoration, recovery, worth
Dutch: warrior
Hopi: willow
Telugu: hand
Welsh: keeper of the keys
Finnish: rejoice

Follow your bliss
your heart
your true nature
With grit
resilience
discernment

Be pragmatic
and poetic
Trust wisely

Waken
to this
one wild and precious life
Take the wheel
and settle into
the journey
Breathe and listen
Learn to dream
with wide eyed joy

I watch you and you are a poem
I hear you and you are a song

My sun
Shine my son
Shine and wax and weave
your dreams between the fragile
filaments of day
and the fibrous husk
of night

Broken Hearted

There are shards
where the heart
is tender, malleable
spiky shards
shifting endlessly in
second and third and fourth
arrows of judgment

Buddha and Kokopelli
must have run
into each other
when Mara came calling
Samsara falling
all around

Be certain that
the heart
will break over
and over and over
over and over
love and
children
species extinction
slavery by many other names
subjugation of immigrants
cultural annihilation
capitalist terrorism
mass shootings
wars for profit
prisons for profit
nuclear holocausts

Heart broken
every second
of every day
must be
the way it's s'posed
to be

Just me and and you
embedded
with shards of heart
Buddha
Kokopelli
and a badger or two

Twilight

come with candles
when the night is
younger than a baby's
first breath

arrangements can be made
with the firmament
to entice

psalms of summer
to resuscitate portals
too long closed
to arable imaginings

first breath
readies the sacraments
of departure

No obelisk too sheer
to scale

with fingers
damp with whim

a child climbs a stool
extends plump palms for washing
nowhere near the sink

The Language of Birds

Ask the stones
how your desires
could have snapped
the backs of winged creatures
flocking to some other
heat
unregistered
in this armored
unrequited
grammar

Spidering along
          some soft pink moan
          some grunting shame
you shaved from your head
in a pillow of night
where you reclined
for an instant

till a falling maple leaf
disturbed you

till the threads of a cobweb
bound you
till a meadowlark's song
troubled you

All this
endangering
the last translator
of the language of birds
who breaks in the moment
between the slap and the child's cry
for you who long
to answer

Kuan Yin
Hearer of the Cries of the World

I am ear
bone and drum, I hear
thrum of flesh on flesh, squall of
babe, howl of
wolf with paw jawed in
steel musings of men, restless
in peace, peaceful in war —
silenced children into
chained-dog whimpers

Your heart aches
in my pulse, your frail
snail self whispers
an inheritance
of laughing gulls, starling whist
the wrist just turned
beneath the razor
meter of milklessly
lapping tongue, limping gait,
clattering beak of wounded owl
rummaging thickets with
the hopeless rustle of a single wing

Answer, I answer
with succoring wind
and strands of hair
to wind in your fist
your infant fist
grasping at mythless roots
with grip too weak to hinder
bone-rattling snips of judgment, lost in
skin, undone as

knots to anchors
hoisted or dropped
invisible as snow geese
with wings turned
towards the sun

Answer, I answer
with lotus
mind tuned
to cliffs scaled with
nails dug into granite
I tune my ear
to your song I
sing you
dance my
voice with peals
of joy
inform the muse
into music
of your own
arms to cradle
your own walls
in the ear
of my ear

After the Concert

On the corner of Sixth and Market
a woman is screaming
long wordless shrieks
for loud terrified minutes.
She screams endlessly
until a man
picks her up
cradles her like
a child.
As we pass she says,
*I guess I just need
a little rest.*

UnNatural Selection

"[Fear of man] is not acquired by individual birds in a short
time, even when much persecuted; but that in the course of suc-
cessive generations it becomes hereditary."
—Charles Darwin, *The Voyage of the Beagle*

Trouble with city living is
everything tends to look Darwinian
beginning and ending with
pigeons
the way they
peck at and walk over
the wounded and sick

Trouble with Darwin
was the way he hurled lizards
into tidepools
to contrive his theories

Amblyrhynchus cristatus
(the lizards in question)
he described as:
"hideous looking creatures
of a dirty black color,
stupid and sluggish in their movements"

Imagine that famous scientist
way out on the Galapagos
flinging lizards
to see what they'd do?

When that poor shell-shocked lizard
who'd never been transmogrified in his life
swam back to old Darwin's feet

he decided
Those lizards are just asking for trouble

And the same theory goes
for urban dwellers
more afraid of starving than those
mean city streets
Standing on the corner
at the feet of some Darwin
bewitched and amazed
at the unnaturally selective
neighborhood quota
of bad luck and death

It's a lizard mind
flicks those channels every day of our lives
knowing it's bad, wrong, lazy and a lie
but easier than confronting the every day
that's in your face
crushing you between its fingers
like devil's food cake

Darwin chased those lizards
to the edge of a cliff
to see if they'd jump
and they wept reptilian tears
in inky nostril squirts
but they wouldn't budge
from that precipice

There's a little girl
who comes to school every day
every day she comes to school
and won't work
and won't listen

and she is cursed into corners
and suspended for impudence

She wrote a story about why tiger roars
  Snake asks why
  Monkey asks why
  Elephant asks, *Tiger, why do you roar*
so loud at night?

But she comes to school every day
because her home is her ocean
where her father drinks a little
too much
comes into her bedroom at night
and roars

We have a lizard brain stem
that's like a light switch
She says it flickers
on   off
on   off

so nothing gets through
that we can't handle

lifting the fallen rose
she said, "I was hoping
I could hang by my thorns"

Family Recipe

There's not much to go on in the files.
It's a military family. Someone tells you what to do all the time.
You get married and the children start coming,
they relocate you so often you lose contact with family and friends.
After a while it's just Christmas cards and birthday presents.

He keeps the guns broken down.
He gets angry when the boys fight, sometimes he hits them.
When the yelling gets too loud she goes into the back room,
makes identical ceramic molds.
She enjoys that.

In the padded room think about how little you know of the family,
how you only see the bruise under her eye,
but only for a moment because the child brings you back.
The child lives in the present.

The room is five by six feet with carpeted walls.
Tell him, "I'm with you. You're safe."
Cross his arms over his chest, hold his wrists, lock his legs under
    yours.
Rock, sing, whisper, but don't let go.
He'll say, "You're hurting me, you're killing me!"
Hold on. Keep your head tilted to one side so he can't hit your chin.
Tell him, "I'm being careful, I'll keep you safe."

When he says he'll burn you up too,
say, "You're remembering the fire."
Don't talk too much. Say, "I'll hold you till you're calm."
He'll scream, "I am calm!"
Don't let go.
Don't say anything.

Wait until his breathing and heartbeat slow.
Wait until the struggling stops.
Let go one arm at a time.
Talk softly and keep your back to the door.

Hold his hand and walk him to his desk. Put a pencil in his hand,
tell him "It's time for math now."
Say, "Good, that's right, you're doing fine."
Stay with him until he forgets you're there.

At night, think about the way he collects bits of brightly colored
  paper,
string, broken glass. The way he calls them his treasure, his jewels.
When you take him to the beach, the way he collects so many shells
they slip through his fingers and fall out of his pockets.
When you buy strawberries, the way he puts one in his pocket
  for his mother.

The way he's always hungry.
The way he brought one whole raw fish between two slices of
  white bread for lunch.

Double Dutch

On buckling playground asphalt
  candy wrappers
  pink bunny barrettes
  headless plastic monsters
  bow-shaped buttons
  melting bubble gum
  donut skid marks
  used condoms and bullets

A salamander
(at first mistaken for a bug)
is ecstatically fondled by 54
nature deprived
six-year-old
hands
until it is finally
loved to death

No slides
  jungle gyms
  swings
  tunnels
  wooden bridges

but beneath three
netless, graffiti-covered backboards
child ghosts
sweat & swear
pound hoops
haunt the streets
fill shopping carts with aluminum cans
or hover about liquor store transoms
where their supple bodies

succumbed to the gun
while our youngest
valiantly continue
to play
  kickball
  four square
  double dutch
  hopscotch

How many little girls
sent to the store for ice cream
survive
behind the dumpster rapes?

How many little boys from
this overcrowded
understaffed
quota driven
text deprived
elementary school
outrun the cold metal
drop top
speaker bump of
this street slumped
tomb?

At 8:10 a.m.
eleven-year-old Damian says
Life stinks, Miss Kimi,
I wish I was dead

Dante tells me
he's going to run away from home
leaves me three suicide notes
in as many weeks

This time, you'll never see me again...
Pigeons coo, tires screech
sirens follow gunshots
and two-inch obituaries
follow hapless youths
on the wrong street
at the wrong time
where all the streets
are the wrong streets
all the time

Outside the smoke-filled
shit scented
teachers' lounge
boys plot to steal a
cellular phone

Two mothers
duke it out in the hallway
tripping over kindergartners
desperately trying to maintain
the straight silent line
Mrs. Miley
worked so hard
to perfect

Seminary gang
14th Street gang
claim school doors, walls
and bathroom windows
their determined signatures defeat
every apathetic
district whitewash
and we dread the night
when they will accidentally meet

on this last, greatly coveted, open
space

At 8:20 a.m.
a task force
of 15 plainclothes police
with rifles
surround the blue house
across the street
as the children are frantically
hustled inside
without breakfast
without baths

My mom was shot in the leg
last night
My auntie was taken to jail
My mom wouldn't let me in
so I slept in a van

An entire third grade class becomes hysterical
when a student describes
his cousin's drive-by death
on their way to school
and a stumbling substitute asks
Who here has known someone
who has died?

I can't remember how many brothers, cousins,
fathers, and uncles were killed this year
but I'm learning
how to skip fast
between the ropes
and keep on
jumping

Pouring
for Susan

It's been a long
day, you look
tired, would you like
a cup of tea?

I can see
by the lines around your
mouth, eyes, color
of your skin
is pale
is white
is the color of votive candles in
Spain, in the
churches there were
glass cases with
wax effigies
of saints
of virgins
dead or sleeping
arms filled with
roses, wearing
satin
smiling, you look
like them, you must be very
tired, have a little
more tea

One morning at school
Maurice came in
growling, yes
growling and looked like he might
bite

and locked himself in the
bathroom while his teacher
stood outside the door saying,

"Having a hard morning, Maurice?
Looks like you're having a hard morning.
Looks like you might need some
tea. Why don't I fix you
a nice cup of
tea?"

There was something
in her voice
that was soothing
that was
careful as
balancing eggs on her
tongue and she
made him
tea and he grew
calm
and wanted to add
and subtract
for her

I used to throw
parties, invite
friends, prepare
chicken with
feta cheese and
spinach, pies
apple and ricotta
and afterwards
I'd say,
"Tea, anyone?"

and I'd steep and grind
pour and say,
"Are you full?
Are you well?
Would you like
some more?"

I pour and it's
enchanted pouring
from long years of
practice, centuries of
sentiment, the
sediment of ancestry
I cannot recollect
but have taken up
like dandelion seed takes root
once the child has
made her wish, so
temporal, it shines on her cheek
for a wingbeat

But I've forgotten
it's tea you're wanting
I'll do the pouring
I've always done the pouring
See how the leaves remain in the cup?
See how I read them
with my eyes
closed?

remember
summer
plums
windfallen apples
the sound of
fruit walking?

Ancestral Sestina

My grandmother was grown in Matsuyama castle
She played the koto
never learned to cook
was a plum blossom child
plucked from a young tree
to marry her sister's widowed husband in America

She grew ten children in America
in California where her home was his castle
watched him graft plum branches to an apricot tree
reminded of the koto
she played as a child
when she wasn't learning to cook

Her daughters learned to cook
hamburgers and tsukemono, American
names for every child
At times she grew distant in the hum of her mind-castle
cried for her koto
clung to her plum tree

Twice felled from her tree
plum rendered with cooking
she surrendered the strains of her koto
to foreclosure by the Bank of America
She burned Matsuyama photos of her rice-paper castle
escaped to Colorado as the camps claimed her children

Roosevelt's imprisoned, epicanthic-eyed children
grew tough and cordial as manzanita trees
grew rock gardens around barren barrack-castles
determined to cook
the meatless bones tossed off by America

without snapping the back of the koto
I have never held a koto
am not a child
of assimilated America
am the apricot branch of the plum tree
an ambivalent cook
in a negligent castle

I imagine the poignant strain of a koto, tuned to the ear of a
paper-walled castle
a petulant child, in need of a cook
who planted a plum tree in the Salinas Valley

Relations

Basho admired moonflowers on his way to the deep north.
In her garden, my aunt points out the prickly globe that blooms
  at night.
Tomiko, child of bountiful harvest, in the year of the windfallen
  outhouse.

Coyote ghost looms
behind the English elm
How spare this winter sun

"The wandering jew is from the Fletchers,
the succulent from Mrs. Manzanola, and
the octopus plant is from 1231 Locust Street.
The people have died so I feel I must keep the plants alive."

O shattered pumpkin
Jack o'lantern grin shivers
face down in the stream

Basho walked the narrow road in sandals and a paper coat.
My samurai ancestors sold their title five hundred years ago.
Their sword keeps its edge in my father's house.

"Dad's carving the turkey. He wasn't too happy
when I backed into the Jaguar.
Dad's carving the turkey, the house is full of Blums,
I'd better go... "

Rabbit in the larkspur
Rabbit in the moon springs clear
Tempering the sword

After the guests leave we eat
shoyu on our pickles, green tea over
white rice, shoyu on our turkey.
My uncle comes home with
blood on his hands, smiles
at his wife, hides
the bird.

Geese stay low after
the moon sets, knowing better than to
fly in the face of the sun

After waking from her nap, my aunt
throws a slipper on the stomach of her still
sleeping husband. His eyes open, undaunted he feels for the soft
blow, solemnly examines her tiny
sole, as though he had been waiting for this shoe to drop.
Retired shoemaker of 43 years.

Basho cries for long dead
warriors, leaves the baby
on the road to die

Sun-webbed flecked
memory: "Grandfather chose a sturdy tree for grafting
one fruit to another – Miraplum?
I don't know – some well-rooted thing..."

Chartreuse fin slices
rippled lake under withered
frown of muddy sky

"Grandmother loved the fields
hated the indoors – maybe that's why
she hated to cook

but she cooled the baked fish
in the bathtub so the flesh
would remain on the bone
to please us..."

Moonflower, larkspur
eleusis, columbine draw
straws, wander the sun

A Harvest of Stars

Dawn's tourniquet binds my jaw
winds down a blind and empty street
argues in strains of apple and oak
that measures
the burning abyss between us

There is no fortune beyond the touch of our fingers
beneath the cloud of your brow I come
sheathed in veils of tourmaline and quartz
my hand my only
weapon
my only gift
What treasure of pulse and flesh do you bring?

Like the Roshi who saw my tears among a hundred sightless
    disciples
none other but you can see me
none other but you
can save me
from the wreck and drone
ploughed in our blood
that disdains the reclamation
and purge
of embrace

I cannot erase our tainted ways
but for you I would shatter
the shaping cell of memory,
unfold my wildest feather
for ephemeral journeys into divine jungles
where we could hunt and pray our sins into scripture
whisper Lucifer's secrets out of our bodies and into the ether

to illumine the thousand masks of raped vision
and flay them with Erato and Calliope

Companions of the flame
make with me an odyssey
and we might fly
into the crystal womb of a phoenix
our hearts all wile and wing